THE MYTHOLOGY LIBRARY

Chinese Myths

Don Nardo

San Diego, CA

For more information, contact:
ReferencePoint Press, Inc.
PO Box 27779
San Diego, CA 92198
www.ReferencePointPress.com

LIBRARY OF CONGRESS CATALOGING-IN-PUBLICATION DATA

Names: Nardo, Don author
Title: Chinese myths / by Don Nardo.
Description: San Diego, CA : ReferencePoint Press, 2026. | Series: The mythology library | Includes bibliographical references and index.
Identifiers: LCCN 2025025039 (print) | LCCN 2025025040 (ebook) | ISBN 9781678212308 library binding | ISBN 9781678212315 ebook
Subjects: LCSH: Mythology, Chinese--Juvenile literature | Tales--China--Juvenile literature
Classification: LCC BL1825 .N374 2026 (print) | LCC BL1825 (ebook) | DDC 299.5/1113--dc23/eng/20250804
LC record available at https://lccn.loc.gov/2025025039
LC ebook record available at https://lccn.loc.gov/2025025040

CONTENTS

MAJOR GODS OF ANCIENT CHINA

Wang-mu + Jade Emperor

Tai-yue
(Protector of People and Animals)

Pangu
(Creator God)

Tian
(God of the Sky)

Kuan-ti
(God of War)

Chang'e
(Moon God)

Caishen
(God of Wealth)

Yan-wang
(God of Death)

Dragon

Yinglong
(Dragon King)

Yellow Dragon*

Pearl Dragon*

Black Dragon*

Long Dragon*

*From the tale "The Four Dragons"

In Harmony with Nature

Long, long ago, according to several popular Chinese legends, an enormous flood devastated the world and almost eradicated humanity. The few, scattered survivors initially had extremely little to eat and desperately sought some sort of dependable food source. That goal was exceedingly difficult to attain because the flood had killed most of the plants that had originally thrived on the earth's surface, including reliable crops like rice. Clearly, people needed to find some surviving seeds that would allow farmers to reestablish the large-scale growing of rice and other staple crops.

When no one could find any such seeds, the surviving residents of China turned to the age-old practice of hunting game with primitive bows. These farmers-turned-hunters employed a dog that had been trained to retrieve game. One fateful day, a flock of birds flew overhead, and the hunters let loose their arrows. When one of the birds was hit, the dog ran into the tall marsh grass and quite easily found the carcass. After picking up the bird, it carried its prize through the grass with its tail sloshing through the mud.

Moments later, the muddy tail caught the attention of one of the hunters. The man alerted his comrades to some small yellow seeds that had stuck to the dog's tail. With growing excitement, the hunters wondered aloud whether those seeds had come from some rice plants that had somehow survived in the marsh. So when the men got back to their village, they planted the seeds. And sure enough, less than a week later, a few tiny rice plants spouted up. Soon, extensive rice crops were planted, and humanity could again rely on agriculture to sustain itself.

MIAO
A local ethnic group mainly inhabiting the mountainous regions of southern China

The Miao people of Southern China perpetuated a similar version of that myth, in which the dog was no less intelligent than humans. Recognizing that its owners were on the brink of starvation, the Miao dog diligently searched for seeds that would facilitate the return of agriculture. During that quest, the dog came upon a hidden path that wound its way up the side of a tall mountain. Scampering along that trail, the dog climbed higher and higher until it reached the lush, green fields that grew on the edges of heaven.

In that spot, three minor nature gods were watering long rows of crops, one of which was clearly rice. The delighted dog prudently waited till the divine gardeners moved on. Then, as quickly

According to Chinese lore, when a massive flood devastated the world, the few survivors desperately searched for food. Thanks to good fortune and a local dog, the people were saved by the discovery of rice seeds that ultimately yielded a bountiful harvest.

as possible, it collected as many rice seeds as it could carry and ran back down the mountain path. In time, those seeds became the basis for the countless rice crops grown and consumed in China in the centuries that followed.

Landscapes Spectacular to Behold

These and other similar myths from ancient China highlight the land's plants and animals. Not only do they explain how crucial aspects of the world and society came to be, but such tales also pay homage to the wonders of nature and emphasize their fundamental importance to humans.

MIAO DOG
The mythical canine that supposedly saved humanity by swiping some rice seeds from heaven

In fact, a large number of ancient Chinese myths incorporate key aspects of nature into their storytelling. Experts suggest that this may be because China's landscape and other natural features are spectacular to behold. The land's well-watered valleys, deep verdant forests, and scenic seacoasts have awed locals and visitors alike. Chinese myths tend to portray people as small, not very consequential beings. "Compared to the other splendors of creation, the mountains and streams, the forests and flowers," write scholars O.B. Duane and N. Hutchison, humans were relegated to a lesser status, though always respectful of nature's bounty. "Never before," they point out, "in any other culture or early literature, was the emphasis on nature and humanity's communion with it, so crucial. [People's] good fortune depended on [their] ability to behave in accordance with the dictates of Heaven. From ancient times onwards, the highest ambition [they] could aspire to was to determine the natural law of things and to behave in sympathy with it."[1]

The belief system of the earliest Chinese reflected a reverence for all aspects of the natural world. The oldest of the country's folktales, says mythologist Te Lin, exhibit "an animistic view of the world . . . in which everything is seen as alive, even rocks and soil." Moreover, in animistic myths, humans "have a quite lowly position. Rather than standing at the center of the cosmos, they are fairly insignificant, taking their place in the natural order. This perspective is echoed in Chinese paintings, where tiny figures are dwarfed by the sweeping vistas of natural features, mountains, and waterfalls."[2]

This tremendous prominence of natural forces in the Chinese myths is not surprising, according to Duane and Hutchison. After all, the earliest Chinese, like primeval peoples around the globe, were amazed by nature's wonders. Thus, the stories preserved that sense of wonder while being "passed by word of mouth by a simple people attempting to explain the origins of the cosmos and other [natural] phenomena beyond their comprehension."[3]

CHAPTER ONE

How the World and People Came to Be

According to a popular Chinese myth, at an unknown point in the distant past, not long after the emergence of the earth and humanity, there lived a resourceful young man named Suirenshi who learned how to make and control fire. This cornerstone of civilization allowed people to warm themselves on cold days, cook their food, and smelt metals to make tools and weapons. Thus, this feat remains a popular and important part of China's earliest origin tales.

Suirenshi's story begins when he heard a rumor that a highly unusual tree could be found deep within China's biggest, least-explored woodland, the Great Forest. It was said that this special tree was covered with sparks of light, a sight that thrilled all who had the good fortune to behold it. The problem was that when Suirenshi mentioned the fabled tree to the residents of his village, they laughed at him. It was only a tall tale, they insisted. Being mocked did not discourage Suirenshi, however. Suspecting that there might be something to the rumor, he filled a cloth sack with food and headed for the Great Forest.

SUIRENSHI
A mythical Chinese innovator who purportedly discovered how to make and control fire

The young man wandered through the woods for several days, hoping to chance upon the mystical sight. He was just about to give up the quest when he came upon an extremely tall tree resting in the center of a large clearing. Suirenshi's eyes widened at the sight of hundreds of woodpeckers energetically stabbing their pointed beaks into the tree's bark. These repeated jabs created bright sparks that together lit up the shadowy glade. Surely, Suirenshi reasoned, this must be the legendary sparkling tree.

For more than two hours the young man was captivated by the glittering display produced by the woodpeckers. And then, quite suddenly, an idea popped into his head. Hurriedly, he searched the clearing until he found a flat, pointed rock that fit comfortably in his hand. Walking to the tree, he started pounding the rock into the tree bark in imitation of the birds' pecking. And that produced a spark.

As the intrepid young man continued pounding, thereby generating one spark after another, one of those slivers of light dropped down onto a dead leaf, which abruptly burst into flame. The intrigued Suirenshi immediately gathered more leaves and repeated the experiment. Eventually, he added sticks to the burning leaves and in that way made the world's first campfire.

According to an oft-told tale, a resourceful young man learned how to make fire by watching hundreds of woodpeckers (not unlike this one) pecking holes in trees.

On returning to his village, Suirenshi showed his discovery to his relatives and neighbors, who were spellbound. They apologized for doubting his story about the special tree and expressed their thanks that they could now keep warm on chilly nights. Furthermore, they later learned to use fire to cook their food and passed that knowledge on to neighboring villages.

China's Sheer Immensity

The story of Suirenshi's pivotal discovery of fire is only one of many ancient Chinese tales about the beginnings of things. In fact, one way that China's myths differ from the origin tales of most of the world's peoples and religions is that China has an unusually large number of creation stories. In comparison, Judaism, Christianity, and Islam, for instance, have one clear-cut tale about how things came to be. In that famous story, a single divine being—God—made the universe, including the earth, in a few days and went on to create plants, animals, and humans.

In contrast, the multiple Chinese foundation myths consist of numerous separate stories, each with a specific creator, who is sometimes divine and other times human. In some cases the human creators were later deified, or officially declared to be divine by China's government. Across several distinct tales, for example, a lone god fashioned the earth's physical aspects, another god then created people, someone else invented agriculture, still another character introduced fishing, Suirenshi discovered fire, and so forth.

The large number of Chinese creation stories, some of which contradict one another, stem from the sheer immensity of ancient China. That land covered a huge portion of the Asian continent and contained many separate ethnic groups. Each group developed its own local myths, including accounts of the creation of the gods themselves. And these groups might never come in contact with each other to reconcile the separate myths into a unified narrative. In the words of mythologists Lihui Yang and Deming An, when looking at the numerous separate local accounts, gods

An Alternate Version of Suirenshi's Story

The ancient Chinese generated several different versions of the story of Suirenshi and his discovery of how to make and utilize fire. In one, promoted by the Han ethnic group, he got the initial idea after he had risen to the lofty position of the country's emperor. As told by modern mythologists Lihui Yang and Deming An, at the time "people still ate only raw foods." But then,

> one day there was a fire in the forest that killed a lot of animals. When the fire ended, Suirenshi found many animals' bodies burned. He picked up a piece of the cooked flesh from one animal's body and tasted it. It was much more delicious than when eaten raw. He then directed other people to pick apart and eat the cooked animal flesh. Everyone enjoyed the tasty meat very much. However, the cooked meat was soon gone.

Suirenshi did not want to wait around for the next forest fire. To acquire more of that blazing substance, therefore, he first tried to get some by journeying to the sun on a bird's back. When that did not work, however, he learned to make fire by striking two stones together.

Lihui Yang and Deming An, *Handbook of Chinese Mythology*. Oxford University Press, 2005, p. 210.

"may be born by a divine father and mother; come from an egg or other object; be created from air or sound; come from another god's corpse; be made by other deities with mud; or may be transformed from a monkey."[4]

Nevertheless, Yang and An are quick to point out that eventually one of the local creation stories became far more popular than the others and thereby came to be accepted by all Chinese. In that tale, the initial stages of creation were instituted by the very first divine being—Pangu. A Chinese scholar named Xu Zheng, who lived in the 200s CE, was the first person to record Pangu's story in writing. But modern experts think the myth itself was at least a few centuries old by that time.

The Sleeping Giant Awakens

Pangu was supposedly responsible for constructing the world's physical features. All the ancient sources agree that he was an extremely large giant, but those accounts differ considerably regarding his physical appearance. According to modern myth teller E.C. Rammel, some ancient writings claim he was "covered in hair or bearskin or leaves, with horns fixed atop his head and either a chisel or a hammer or an egg in his hand. Other tales speak of a Pangu as a creature from heaven that had the head of a dog and the body of a man."[5]

Appearance aside, Pangu was said to have emerged from a massive primordial egg. As for exactly where that object came from, the ancient accounts are largely mute; perhaps it had always existed, or maybe an early Chinese writing that explained its origin was lost over the centuries. In any case, Pangu laid sleeping inside the egg for eighteen thousand years, and then, in an instant, he woke up.

An eighteenth-century artist depicts Pangu, the creator and first divine being in Chinese mythology, holding the cosmic egg from which he was said to have emerged.

The Five August Emperors

In addition to Shennong, Suirenshi, Nuwa, and Fuxi, the ancient Chinese recognized a few other mythic creators of differing aspects of human culture. Among them were five men collectively called the August Emperors. The earliest of the group, Huang-di, also known as the Yellow Emperor, was said to have ruled the country in the mid-2000s BCE. However, China did not have an organized imperial government that early, so he and the other August Emperors were almost certainly mythical.

Huang-di was credited with the development of astronomy, mathematics, and new measuring instruments for architects and builders. The second member of the group, Zhuanxu, was said to have introduced several religious reforms. And the next August Emperor, Zhuanxu's nephew Ku, purportedly championed music and invented several musical instruments. The fourth ruler in the group—Ku's son Yao—was renowned as a gifted politician who managed to unite many of China's many ethnic groups and clans. Myths claim that Yao also handpicked his successor, Shun, the last of the August Emperors. Shun supposedly convinced most Chinese to work together efficiently to build a peaceful, prosperous society.

Once conscious, Pangu was annoyed that nothing existed outside his cosmic egg. He quickly became determined to fill that void with various kinds of things he would create on his own. First, he had to find a way to break out of the egg, so he imagined an ax in his mind, and a second later an ax appeared in his hand. With it he chopped his way out, and the broken egg supplied the raw materials for his creation project. The egg's lighter elements floated upward and became the sky, while the heavier parts sank downward and formed the earth's solid surface.

After that, Pangu began creating his world, working day and night, without food or rest, for another eighteen thousand years. All that tireless toil quite naturally exhausted him, and when spent, he simply laid down and died. Yet even in death, his wave of creation continued. University of Oxford professor Tao Tao Liu Sanders says that the various parts of his enormous body became building materials for the still expanding environment. His final breaths morphed into the clouds and winds, for example. And his big, booming voice became thunder. In addition, "his left eye turned into the sun and his right eye into the moon. His body and limbs turned into mountain ranges and his blood became flowing rivers. Every part of his anatomy became part of nature. The hairs on his body turned into trees and flowers, the parasites living on his skin turned into animals and fishes."[6]

How Humans Entered Pangu's World

Thanks to Pangu, the earth's landforms, the heavens above, and plants and animals came into being. However, the grand process of creation was not complete, for the crowning glory of that process—humans—did not yet exist. The ancient Chinese had numerous explanations for the arrival of humanity, because diverse ethnic groups in different regions of the country developed their own origin narratives. Those local stories, say Yang and An, variously claimed that humans were "sown from seeds; that they were spat out from the mouths of gods, and goddesses; that they were made from sound; that they were created by two gods touching their knees together . . . that they were created by the sun; or that they were made from the corpse of a divine creature."[7]

NUWA
A Chinese goddess who is credited with fashioning the human race

As it turned out, one of the local versions of humanity's origin—initially introduced by the largest Chinese ethnic group, the Han—became the most widely accepted one. That myth begins with the conversion of mighty Pangu's body into the constituent elements of the natural world. That huge transformation, the early Han people claimed, took a long time—several centuries at least. And during that interval, high above in the sky, a recurring series of miracles took place. To this day, no one can say for sure how these happened, but every few years a divine being suddenly sprang fully formed into existence.

At first, these new deities simply floated from one place to another, with little or no purpose. But then one of them, the goddess Nuwa, looked down on the earth's surface and was awestruck at the majesty and beauty of what Pangu had accomplished. Nevertheless, Nuwa reasoned, something was missing. There were no mortal beings to inhabit the earth's surface, giving it a purpose. She therefore decided to fashion such beings herself, though she did not model them on her physique, which was commonly portrayed as a human head (and sometimes torso) on a serpent's body.

Nuwa chose to make those creatures, which she called humans, from the nutrient-rich soil lining the banks of China's Yellow River. Scooping up globs of the moist mud, she started shaping each into a human body. The goddess was quite happy with the look of the first few people she sculpted, but it soon became clear that this process was taking too long. To speed it up, she rolled a large shaft of sugarcane in the mud and proceeded to vigorously shake it above a patch of dry land. That caused dozens of small drops of mud to rain down, each of which rapidly transformed into a person. Later, to speed up the process even more, the goddess gave the new beings the ability to have children. "Eventually," Sanders writes, "having created enough men and women, Nuwa instituted marriage among them so that they could procreate and continue the human race without any further help from her."[8]

The Formation of Human Culture

According to the ancient Chinese myths, Pangu's and Nuwa's achievements, though crucial, did not account for all of creation. Other gods aided in that wondrous process, developing diverse aspects of human culture, such as the establishment of religion, agriculture, literacy, metalworking, arts and crafts, and systems of law and order.

Of those divine beings who brought cultural enhancements to humanity, one of the most noteworthy was Fuxi. Some ancient tales claim the serpent-bodied Fuxi was Nuwa's brother; others call him her husband. Whatever their relationship, Fuxi was said to have taught people how to hunt, fish, and raise domestic

Shennong is the mythic character credited with introducing agriculture to China. Through his knowledge of plants—especially the use of herbs for healing—he has also been described as the father of Chinese medicine.

animals. Supposedly, he also introduced the art of writing and showed humans how to make copper coins.

Another important divine cultural benefactor was Shennong. His name means "spirit farmer," and he is credited with introducing agriculture to the ancient Chinese. Not only did he invent the hoe and plow for humanity, he also built the first marketplaces in which humans bought and sold food and other goods.

According to myth, Shennong also studied plants, in particular herbs that could be used to heal the sick. A surviving ancient

SHENNONG
One of China's early cultural innovators, he was said to have introduced agriculture to humanity

document states that "he tried the flavor of all the plants . . . letting people know what to avoid or accept. At that time he suffered poisoning seventy times a day."[9] Thereby, Shennong was seen as the father of Chinese medicine.

As mythic innovators, Shennong, Fuxi, and Nuwa performed tremendously vital services for humankind. Together they are known as the Three Divine Sovereigns (or in some parts of China, the Three Sage Kings). Along with Pangu, Suirenshi, and a few others, they are remembered as the divine forces that made the world and human society possible.

A Vast Pantheon of Divine Beings

One of the most popular myths among the ancient Chinese told of how a mortal princess transformed into the awesome, widely beloved goddess of mercy and kindness. Princess Miao Shan was the daughter of Miao Zhuang, a cruel, power-hungry ruler of an early Chinese kingdom. When the princess reached her late teens, her father sought to marry her off to a humorless nobleman who was three times her age. But the normally mild-mannered Miao Shan boldly refused to assent to the marriage. Instead, she told her father that she desired to enter a Buddhist nunnery and devote her life to prayer and good deeds.

MIAO SHAN
The Chinese princess who eventually became Guan-Yin, goddess of mercy

Miao Zhuang saw his daughter's reaction as a display of insolence. Angry with her, he forbade her from becoming a nun. However, she remained stubborn, and eventually her father relented. Nevertheless, to punish her for her impudence, he secretly told the nunnery's mother superior to make the girl's life there as miserable as possible.

What neither the king nor the mother superior realized, however, was that the gods had been watching Miao Shan since her birth, and they greatly admired her. They proceeded to thwart every mean-spirited act of the mother superior. When that older woman told Miao Zhuang that his daughter was thriving rather than suffering, he flew into a rage. Summoning some soldiers, he ordered them to burn down the nunnery; yet once again the gods intervened, this time by sending a rainstorm to put out the flames.

Finally, the king could take no more and condemned his own daughter to death. Yet again, the gods came to her rescue. According to modern myth teller Tony Allan:

> When the executioner tried to behead the girl, his sword shattered. A lance thrust at her broke into pieces. Eventually, she was strangled by a silken cord, but the moment her soul left her body a huge tiger appeared from nowhere and carried off the corpse to a nearby pine forest. The beast was actually a local god in disguise, sent by the [gods] to keep the body unharmed and . . . protect it from decay.[10]

When Princess Miao Shan dared to oppose her father, the king, he ordered her execution. At the moment of her death, a god disguised as a tiger carried her lifeless body to the afterlife.

In the months and years that followed, the gods acknowledged that Miao Shan's compassionate personality made her an excellent candidate for the job of goddess of mercy. And thereafter, taking a new name, Guan-Yin, she happily watched human affairs unfold. Anytime she saw extreme suffering, she did her best to intervene and relieve such misery. A real test of that commitment came when her father contracted a serious disease that caused his entire body to constantly and painfully convulse. Considering the way he had treated her in the past, she could have simply let him suffer. But her sense of kindness and decency outweighed any grudge she may have had. She made sure that her father regained his health, and he was so moved by that gesture that he abdicated the throne and spent the rest of his days helping the poor and needy.

The Heavenly Government

The myth of Miao Shan's ascendancy to godhood is just one of many divine origin stories. China's pantheon, or group of gods, is diverse and innumerable. No one knows how many Chinese deities have been worshipped over the centuries. Allan says that "to this day no one has ever tried to catalogue all these multifarious [diverse] deities, which varied [in number] from place to place."[11] Similarly, not all gods achieved divinity in the same way. Some, like Pangu and Nuwa, mysteriously appeared, seemingly out of nothingness. Others were physically created by existing gods, and still others, like Guan-Yin, were mortal humans who were eventually deified, or transformed into gods.

Because the ancient Chinese saw a divine presence in nearly everything, the gods oversaw virtually every aspect—large or small—of both the natural world and human society. Keeping track of so many deities was challenging, so as the pantheon became standardized during the Han dynasty (206 BCE to 220 CE), Chinese leaders began categorizing many of those deities in the same manner that the government classified people and their political and social roles. Indeed, Allan writes, the Chinese

YU DI
Frequently called the Jade Emperor, he was the leader of the Chinese pantheon of gods

"modeled the divine hierarchy [ladder with levels of importance] directly on the political world they knew, providing Heaven with an emperor, minsters, and minor officials just like China itself."[12]

The leader of that heavenly government bureaucracy was Yu Di, commonly called the Jade Emperor. It was said that he had begun as a human emperor, but during his reign he ruled so wisely and fairly that all the country's residents agreed he had achieved perfection. As a reward, the story went, Chinese political and religious leaders deified him and gave him awesome authority as ruler of all the gods.

The deities in Yu Di's heavenly hierarchy constituted nothing less than a divine civil service. "There were court officials," Allan explains, "such as the Transcendent Dignitary, a sort of celestial doorkeeper. There were masters of the elements, including a Count of the Winds and a Lord of Lightning. One particularly . . . powerful deity was the bird-bearded Thunder God, who was responsible for punishing serious crimes."[13]

The Duke of Thunder Returns a Favor

That divine punisher, Lei Kung, was also often referred to as the Duke of Thunder. Like the many other gods in charge of various niches of the natural world, he appeared in some key myths that were told and retold over the centuries. Perhaps the most popular one demonstrated that, although he forcefully chastised lawbreakers, he could be quite friendly to those who had committed no crimes.

The story begins with a young farmer chopping wood beside his modest house near the edge of a large forest. Hearing claps of thunder in the distance, he reasoned that lightning might strike, so he took shelter beside the trunk of a massive tree. Sure enough, a bolt of lightning did appear, but it struck that very tree, which started to topple over. It just so happened that Lei Kung

Lei Kung is known both as the divine punisher and the Duke of Thunder. He makes thunder with a hammer and drums to chase away evil spirits and punish lawbreakers.

was passing by at the time, and he could not escape the falling tree, becoming ensnared in its tangle of branches.

Seeing the farmer standing a few feet away, the Duke of Thunder politely requested that he come to his aid. The young man was happy to oblige. Employing his trusty ax, he vigorously chopped away the branches until Lei Kung had been freed. The thunder deity then heartily thanked the farmer for kindly rendering aid and flew away into the sky.

It was about a year later that Lei Kung and the farmer had a second encounter. One night the young man went to a nearby town and had too much to drink. Unable to control himself, he

New Religions Shape Chinese Beliefs

During the era when the first emperors ruled China (ca. 1600–1500 BCE), the Chinese had a simple folk religion. The people believed in, prayed to, and made food offerings to various gods. Later, however, three new faiths entered China—Taoism, Confucianism, and Buddhism. And each profoundly affected both people's beliefs and the creation of new myths. Taoism, for instance, advocated that people live in harmony with both nature and the gods, and Taoist-inspired myths reflect that concept. Confucianism, meanwhile, stressed the idea that both citizens and their leaders should maintain high ethical standards. Confucianist-inspired myths therefore tend to depict gods setting moral examples for humans. Finally, Buddhism also encouraged ethical behavior and suggested that right actions could potentially overcome human suffering. As a result, many Buddhist-inspired myths feature gods who teach moral lessons. Remarkably, the three new belief systems, along with the older folk religion, complimented rather than contradicted one another. The four systems blended, producing an outlook on life that put less importance on worshipping the gods and more on how people should lead honest, moral, and productive lives. A great many Chinese myths inherited that overall philosophy.

ran through the streets, threatening bodily harm to everyone who crossed his path. Not surprisingly, the local authorities hauled him to jail. And when he sobered up, he prayed to the Duke of Thunder, hoping that the god would come to his rescue as the farmer had previously done for Lei Kung.

Fortunately for the farmer, Lei Kung did hear that plea. Remembering how the lad had freed him from the fallen tree, he hurried to the town and proceeded to return the favor. As O.B. Duane and N. Hutchison tell it, the god "thundered through the air so loudly that the windows of the courthouse were shattered by the noise. Cowering to the floor in terror, the [judge] ordered the youth to be released."[14] After gaining his freedom, the farmer profusely thanked the Duke of Thunder, and the two remained fast friends for the remainder of the man's long life.

The Scary Deity of Death

In addition to the Jade Emperor, Nuwa, Guan-Yin, and Lei Kung, the divine bureaucracy featured many other major gods who controlled natural forces or presided over social interactions. Yu Shi served as goddess of the rain, which made harvests plentiful. Mazu was goddess of the seas but also protected the fishers who reaped its bounty. As for human relations, Caishen was the deity associated with money and wealth, Yue Lao brought lovers together, Zao Shen reigned as guardian of the home and family, and Kuan-Ti was a deified general who oversaw victories in war.

Although these, along with the other leading deities, were seen as important in one way or another, few of them wielded as much power and influence as the deity of death and the afterlife. Deriving from a Hindu god, Yan Wang—sometimes called Lord Yama and King Yan–was embraced by the Chinese when Buddhism spread across the border from India in the first two centuries CE.

YAN WANG
The Chinese god of death and the afterlife

Much of Yan Wang's strong grip on the popular imagination derived from his frightening appearance. Chinese artists usually depicted him with red skin, bulging eyes, and a lengthy black beard. He was always accompanied by an entourage of menacing characters. One was a scribe (someone skilled at reading and writing), who carried a mystical list of the birth and death dates of all humans, past, present, and future. Yan was also attended by two creepy enforcers named Horse-Face and Ox-Head. Among their duties was to bring the souls of recently deceased people to Yan, who judged them, separating the sinners from the innocent.

The punishments that Yan Wang inflicted on the souls of sinners were gruesome. Thieves and arsonists were crucified, for example. Meanwhile, murderers were stabbed dozens of times, liars were tossed off tall bridges, merchants who cheated their customers were hung on big hooks until they bled to death or died of starvation, and adulterers had their bodies cut in half by large saws.

Even if a human soul was innocent, it might be condemned if it made the mistake of lying to that god. Yan hated liars, as one

The Popular Deity of Wealth

One of the most prevalent of the many deities in the ancient Chinese pantheon was Caishen, the god of money and wealth. Moreover, says historical writer Emily Mark, that deity remains widely popular among Chinese people today. Statues of him, she writes,

> can be seen in businesses run by Chinese merchants all around the world and in Chinese homes. His statue shows a wealthy man seated in a silk robe holding riches in both hands. He is sometimes accompanied by two attendants carrying bowls of gold. He was not just the god of material wealth but of a rich life which meant a happy family and a secure, prosperous, and respectable job. Caishen was very generous to his followers but was not foolish and did not give out his wealth to just anyone. People had to prove themselves worthy of his generosity by working hard, praying to him regularly, and thanking him for his gifts. Temples and shrines to Caishen were probably the most numerous in ancient China.

Emily Mark, "Most Popular Gods & Goddesses of Ancient China," *World History Encyclopedia*, April 25, 2016. www.worldhistory.org.

of his best-known mythical tales illustrates. As that story begins, Yan was sitting on his throne, listening as his attendants read out the accounts of a long line of souls waiting for judgment. When a soldier's soul reached the front of the line, Ox-Head accused him of committing various crimes, including slaughtering some children while attacking a city. Yan interrupted and asked the soldier why he had slain the children. Instead of answering the question honestly, the soldier claimed he had never done a single thing wrong in his entire life. Knowing full well this was a lie, Yan became enraged. The death deity snapped his fingers, and out of nowhere appeared a gigantic hand covered with sharp metal spikes. When the god snapped his fingers a second time, the hand repeatedly pounded the soldier, turning him into a ghastly pile of broken bones and shredded flesh. Such was the type of punishment that discouraged living souls from acting dishonestly or spreading falsehoods.

Numerous Local Gods

Over time, major deities such as Yan Wang, the Jade Emperor, and Lei Kung became recognized and worshipped by people all over China. Yet there were also numerous minor gods that still populated the local myths of China's various regions. Small pockets of ethnic groups were distributed throughout China, each existing in a separate river valley, mountain slope, or strip of seacoast. Many of these locales tended to retain their own social customs, rules, and gods.

The vast host of local deities were viewed as formless spirits that inhabited specific geographic areas or even parts of the home. There were household spirits, for example, who were thought to protect the family from harm. These included a guardian of the front door, an overseer of the bedrooms, a protector of parents, and a spirit who supposedly helped the husband and

The kitchen god Zao Shen, depicted with his wife, oversaw the happiness and prosperity of Chinese families. According to myth, Zao Shen's reports to the Jade Emperor led to either reward or punishment for each family.

father achieve success in his job. Also, just outside the home lurked spirits called Kuei Shen. As historical writer Emily Mark writes, these manifested as "nature spirits, who might inhabit a tree or live by a stream or preside over a garden."[15]

Arguably the most crucial of all domestic spirits was the kitchen deity, Zao Shen. In addition to making sure that food storage and preparation proceeded smoothly, he was said to oversee the family's overall happiness and prosperity. Each month, Mark explains, he "left the home to report to the local gods and spirits on the family's conduct. If they had behaved well, he was instructed to increase their riches and happiness; if they had behaved badly, he was told to withdraw riches and happiness. 'Riches' meant not only material wealth but comfort and well-being, which was further assured by his warding off evil spirits."[16]

Historians and mythologists find it fascinating that belief in these local spirits did not die out as the modern world emerged from the ancient and medieval eras. Mark points out that worship of these minor deities was labeled superstitious and forbidden when the Communist Party came to power in China in 1949. However, "they continued to be worshipped privately by the people and are still honored in many [Chinese] homes all over the world today,"[17] says Mark.

CHAPTER THREE

Timeless Tales of Mythic Lovers

There is an old saying among the Chinese that in its solitary journey across the night sky, the moon feels terribly sad. The goddess who personifies that heavenly orb, Chang'e, is also extremely lonely, people say. Year after year, and century after century, she yearns in her heart to recapture a long-lost love.

That story, which every Chinese child learns by the age of six or seven, begins deep in the mists of time, in an era when the earth was still young and no moon yet traversed the sky each night. In that bygone age, Chang'e was a young human married to an expert archer named Hou Yi. Most often called simply Yi, he had earlier carried out several successful military missions for the reigning emperor, Yao.

HOU YI
A famous soldier and archer who married and later lost the moon goddess Chang'e

At the time, although no moon yet existed, ten suns marched across the sky each day. Not surprisingly, that made the earth's surface exceedingly hot, and over time farmers' crops steadily withered, causing severe food shortages. Worried that everyone might starve to death, Yao decided that something drastic must be done. Recalling Yi's past exploits, the emperor asked the great archer to try to save humanity.

Accepting this new mission, Yi grasped his trusty bow and arrows. And in a superhuman display of strength and skill, he proceeded to shoot down nine of the ten suns. For saving humankind, a powerful nature goddess rewarded Yi with a special gift. It was a little green pill that would transform anyone who swallowed it into an immortal heavenly being.

After thanking the goddess, Yi went home to his beloved Chang'e and showed her the pill. She should not worry, he said, for he had decided never to swallow it. Doing so would transform him into a god, he explained, and that would oblige him to live in heaven and leave her behind to grow old and die. That, he said, was something he simply could not bring himself to do.

Chang'e thanked her husband for expressing his deep love for her. And their lives went on happily during the months that followed. However, one day Chang'e had a brief moment of weakness. Unable to fight off an overpowering feeling of curiosity about the effects of the pill, she swallowed it. In Tony Allan's words, "At once an extraordinary sense of lightness came over her. Escaping the pull of gravity, she found herself helplessly drawn upwards. Yi saw her plight, but was at a loss to know what was happening. . . . Too late, he tried to seize [her], but she was already well beyond his reach, soaring heavenwards at an ever-faster rate."[18]

Within a mere few hours, Chang'e became the moon and was forever separated from the love of her life. Until his dying day, Yi sadly longed for her. And during the countless centuries that have elapsed since that fateful day, the story goes, she has no less longed for him.

A Great Many Tales of Love

For uncountable centuries the Chinese have retold the story of the lost love of Chang'e and Hou Yi. Perhaps not content with the mournful account, some Chinese storytellers have also passed along an alternate myth that provides a somewhat less sad ending to the tale. In it, Yi tries to follow his lost wife into the heavens and manages to reach the castle of a sky god. That deity takes pity on him and gives him the ability to visit Chang'e once a month, although unfortunately she can never visit him. This is the origin of the well-known Chinese adage that the sun shines on the moon, yet the moon cannot shine on the sun.

The story of Chang'e and Hou Yi is one of many tales of fortunate or doomed lovers within Chinese mythology. "There are literally

After swallowing the pill of immortality, the once-mortal Chang'e flies up to the heavens. As a result of her rash act, she becomes the moon goddess and is forever separated from the love of her life, her husband Hou Yi.

hundreds of love stories in Chinese culture," remarks an editor for the major news outlet *China Daily*. This is because "Chinese people adore love stories and have communally passed down many ancient tales of romance and love through the generations."[19]

Unlike many Western narratives that emphasize the notion of "true love" bringing lovers together, mythic Chinese couples did not always find each other through fate. This may be due to the fact that most early Chinese marriages were arranged by parents or other relatives. Many couples initially entered loveless marriages, even when they were lucky enough to develop feelings for each other later. Certainly, modern Chinese mythologist Yang Tingting points out, "in the highly regimented and gendered world of ancient China, being romantic was not always easy." Nevertheless, she adds, true romantic love did sometimes exist. Some couples "were devoted to each other to the end, and were moved to perform selfless acts for love. Many stories of romantic couples from ancient [Chinese] history are still well-known today, recited as a reminder of the power of the heart."[20]

A Festival to Honor Chang'e

The famous myth in which a maiden named Chang'e transforms into the moon continues to be told and retold by each successive generation of Chinese. So popular is that tale that over the years the country developed a traditional public holiday to honor that goddess. That special celebration, known as the Mid-Autumn Festival, is held annually across China. Most of the holiday activities are based on a key detail of the story. In it, after losing Chang'e, her husband Hou Yi hoped that she might someday, somehow, return to the earth. So once a year he dutifully left samples of her favorite desserts and fruits out in an open field. Likewise, during the Mid-Autumn Festival the Chinese meet in fields and place various foodstuffs on small altars. They also enjoy cookouts and other feasts of their own. The yearly festivity has evolved into a celebration of the family and friends in each person's life.

Tragedy at the Great Wall

The myth of Chang'e's and Hou Yi's lost love shows that the power of the heart can indeed be great, even when the relationship ends tragically. Another well-known Chinese myth that vividly illustrates that point is the story of a young woman named Meng Jiang and a young man from her village, named Fan. The couple fell deeply in love and got married. For the first year of their union, they were blissfully content and looked forward to a lifetime of happiness.

MENG JIANG
A Chinese woman whose husband died while working as a laborer on China's Great Wall

At the start of the marriage's second year, however, some government officials seized Fan and some of the village's other male citizens to work on the huge structure that came to be called the Great Wall of China. The men ended up more than 100 miles (161 km) away from their homes and their loved ones. At first, Fan wrote Meng Jiang a letter every few weeks, but then those messages ceased. Hearing rumors that large numbers of the workers were starving to death, Meng made a momentous decision. She gathered some food and other essentials and trekked overland toward the wall.

When the courageous young woman reached the construction site, she questioned several of the workers about Fan's whereabouts. One laborer responded that he had known Fan, who, sad to say, had recently died from overwork and exhaustion. His body, the worker added, lay somewhere within a finished section of the wall.

Shocked and overcome with grief, Meng clenched her fists and pounded on the Great Wall. As she did so, hundreds of workers supported her by wailing loudly in honor of Fan. Soon, it appeared that nature's forces joined in, as lightning bolts struck the wall and gale-forced winds picked up trees and hurled them at the structure. Then, suddenly, a large section of the wall shook violently and collapsed, spewing broken stones far and wide. As Meng approached the wreckage, she came upon Fan's body. Carefully, she carried the corpse to a high cliff overlooking the sea and jumped. As the two bodies disappeared beneath the waves, one of the workers commented that thereafter Meng and Fan would always be together in death, as they should have been in life.

In a tale of lost love, a newly married woman searches for her husband, who has disappeared while working on the Great Wall of China. She is so distraught when she finds his body that she carries him to a cliff and jumps into the sea.

The Star Lovers and the Queen Mother

Despite these examples, not all ancient Chinese love stories end in death or separation. In some myths about love, the main characters were able to overcome their problems and find ultimate happiness. One of the more famous tales of this kind—a perennial favorite among modern Chinese of all ages—is the story of Niu Lang and Zhi Nu.

The story begins in a half-forgotten age not long after the earth's creation, when godlike beings, similar to the angels envisioned in Christianity, occupied the sky's brightest stars. The star Vega, for example, was inhabited by a female being named Zhi Nu, and the star Altair was home to a male entity called Niu Lang. The two met in the summer night sky and fell in love. At first, however, they decided to keep their relationship a secret because a powerful sky goddess commonly called the Queen Mother disapproved of romances among star beings.

Unfortunately for the lovers, the Queen Mother did find out their secret and punished them by stripping them of their status. Zhi Nu remained in the sky but became a cloud weaver, a minor nature spirit who decided what shapes clouds would take. As for Niu Lang, he became a lowly human cowherd in a small village on the earth.

For a few years the lovers were unable to meet and missed each other terribly. But they were not fated to be separated forever. One day the Queen Mother allowed Zhi Nu and a few other minor nature deities to visit the earth and swim in a pond in a picturesque woodland. That forest happened to be fairly near Niu Lang's humble cottage, where he lived a modest life with an aging, talking cow that had become his only friend. On a sunny afternoon the cow told him that he should go to the pond, where he would see some angelic creatures swimming. One of those beings, the cow said, would eventually become Niu Lang's wife.

Sure enough, when Niu Lang reached the pond, he saw his beloved friend Zhi Nu. The two joyfully embraced. And wasting no time, they got married, and she moved into his cottage, which they continued to share with the faithful cow.

The Cow's Secret

One day, however, the cow took Niu Lang aside and told him it would soon die of old age. Moreover, the creature said, it had been keeping a secret for a long time. It too had once inhabited a star in the sky until the Queen Mother had, in anger, turned it into an earthly cow. While on earth, the cow went on, it had done its best to look after its former fellow star spirits, Niu Lang and Zhi Nu. It instructed Niu Lang to make a coat out of its hide after its passing; the coat, the cow said, would act like a sail and allow Niu Lang to follow his love back to the heavens on a strong wind.

Niu Lang followed the orders, and the lovers were able to return to the stars together, where some sympathetic birds built a bridge connecting Vega and Altair. Meanwhile, centuries later, on earth, the modern Chinese kept alive the ancient story of the night sky lovers by incorporating them into an annual holiday. Often called Chinese Valentine's Day by residents of other nations,

The Old Man in the Moonlight

One popular Chinese myth featuring Yue Lao, the god of love, involves a farmer named Wei. One evening, Wei was taking a stroll in the moonlight when he chanced upon an old man reading a book. Wei had no idea that the old man was Yue Lao in disguise. When Wei inquired what the old man was reading, the god answered that it was a list of all future marriages. After being told that Wei himself was in the book, Wei was convinced the old man was senile.

Pointing down the road at a little girl walking with her father, the old man said that the girl would grow up to become Wei's wife. To prove the prediction false, Wei produced a knife, stabbed the girl in the back, and ran away. Fifteen years later, Wei met a woman he liked and proposed marriage. On their wedding night, he noticed a large scar on her back. When questioned, she said that many years before, a strange man had suddenly stabbed her in the back. Wei now realized that the old man in the moonlight had told the truth. Luckily for Wei, his new bride turned out to be a loving, faithful wife.

it features a celebration in which people get together, eat a meal, and use telescopes to view Vega, Altair, and other stars. According to Victoria Ma of San Jose, California's Chinese Historical & Cultural Project, "Some common foods during this holiday are sweet pastries, confectionaries, candies, and fruits. In some places, people [build] a four-meter-long bridge with incense sticks and decorate them with flowers, like the bridge in the legend. Watching the bridge burn in the dark night, they [wish] for love and happiness in life."[21]

The Strongest Force in Nature

For generations the people of China have viewed the myth of Niu Lang and Zhi Nu as one of the country's four most cherished love stories. Another tale in that group—often called "The White Snake"—features a lead character named Bai Suzhen. Over a thousand years old, she was the spirit of a snake who was able to assume human form at will.

In the story, Bai Suzhen happened upon a kindhearted young man named Xu Xian. The two fell in love at first sight and soon got married. The snake spirit did love her new husband with all her heart, but she decided not to reveal her identity for fear that he might reject her.

Eventually, however, Xu Xian did find out the truth. A nosy local monk secretly investigated Bai Suzhen and discovered she was not a human but an ancient white snake. Bent on exposing her, he tricked her into drinking a potion that reversed her transformation process. After she and Xu went to bed one night, she turned back into a snake. And the next morning, when he saw her true form, he fell into a coma-like state and could not be awakened.

XU XIAN
The husband of the maiden Bai Suzhen, he initially did not know she was the disguised spirit of a snake

Fortunately for Xu, Bai Suzhen acted heroically. Alternating between snake and human form, she searched through the known world and found a magical herb that made him regain consciousness. So deep was his love for her that he came to accept her despite her original form. And the couple went on to enjoy a long, happy life together. Among the Chinese, this and other similar tales celebrate something known to a fortunate few around the globe—that true love is surely the strongest force in nature.

CHAPTER FOUR

Celebrated Warriors and Other Heroes

At various points in ancient China's long history, unusually skilled warriors fought in the ranks of the country's armies. For one reason or another, most of them never became well known. And not surprisingly, those who did were remembered for centuries after their deaths. Likewise, not all of China's national heroes who earned eternal fame for their exploits were warriors. Some earned the title for discovering something important or contributing to the advancement of some aspect of Chinese culture.

Meanwhile, a chosen few of China's mythical heroes combined uncommon military skills with other noteworthy deeds. And high on that short list was the legendary Huang-di, also known as the Yellow Emperor. It was said that he ruled for at least a century and that he was a great inventor who introduced the first large seagoing vessels, various musical instruments, and the calendar.

Huang-di was even more renowned for his military exploits. When he was a young man, the story goes, he ruled half of central China, while a competing ruler, known as the Red Emperor, held sway in the other half. A talented general, Huang-di fought many battles against the Red Emperor before soundly defeating him to rule over all of China's central region.

Although Huang-di desired peace with neighboring peoples, he soon found himself drawn into another war. At the time, in the arid, desolate lands situated along China's southwestern border, there lived a warlike people ruled by a king named Chi-you. Half human and half monster, he was physically hideous, emotionally disturbed, and power hungry. Eager to conquer all of China and make its people slaves, he raised a large army and invaded central China.

To meet this challenge, Huang-di gathered an army of his own—one that was amazingly innovative. It included not only human soldiers but also bears, tigers, and the ghosts of many deceased Chinese. The two immense forces clashed in a battle that lasted several days. Realizing he was losing, Chi-you resorted to the dishonorable tactic of casting a magic spell that enveloped the Chinese army in dense fog. It "swirled around them, completely

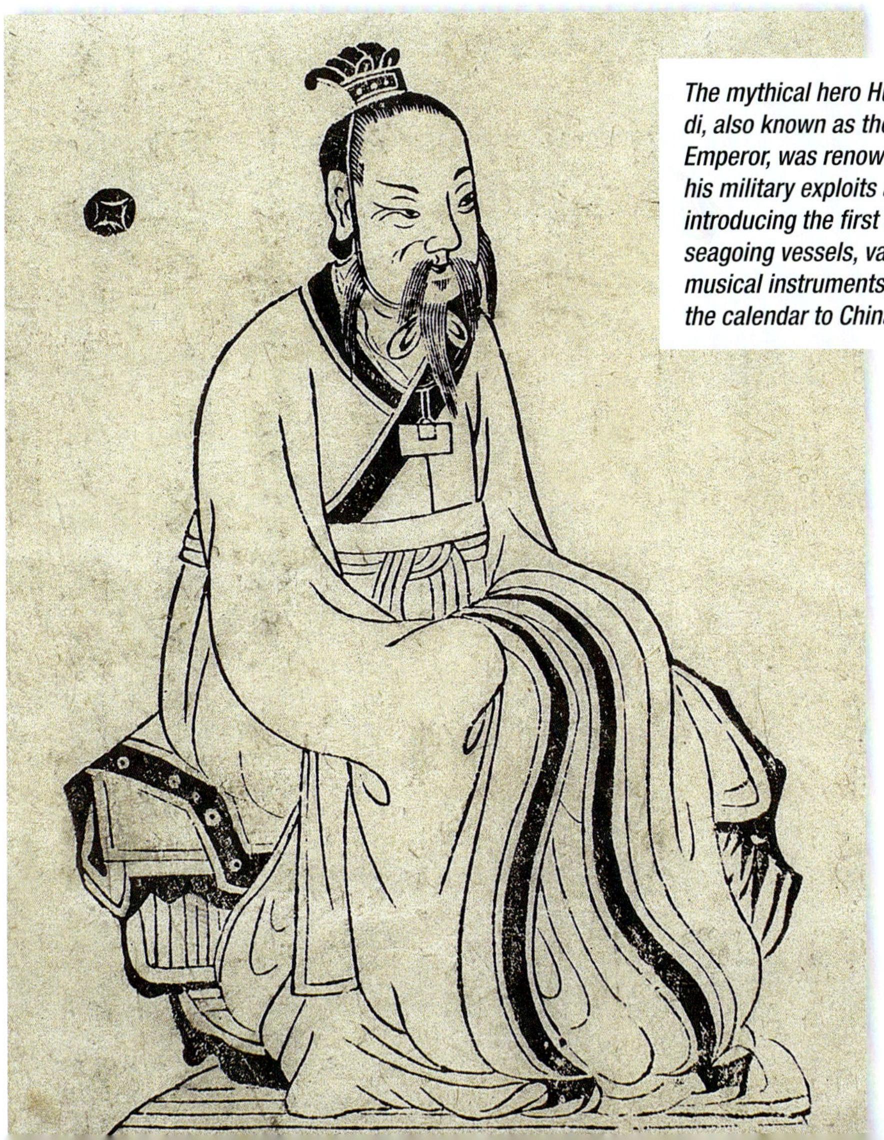

The mythical hero Huang-di, also known as the Yellow Emperor, was renowned for his military exploits and for introducing the first large seagoing vessels, various musical instruments, and the calendar to China.

obscuring their vision," O.B. Duane and N. Hutchison write, "and they began to stab blindly with their weapons at the thin air. Then suddenly, the wild animals who made up a large part of the emperor's forces started to panic and to flee in every direction."[22]

Huang-di knew he had to quickly find some way to counteract the fog. It suddenly struck him that what was needed was a device that could show his fighters which direction to take to reach clear skies. In less than an hour, with the aid of a minor god named Feng-Hou, Huang-di invented the compass. With it, the Chinese escaped the fog and defeated and drove away Chi-you's army. Later, Huang-di captured and executed that evil adversary, and not long afterward the heroic Yellow Emperor climbed onto the back of a huge dragon, which carried him upward into heaven.

A modern-day statue celebrates the kindhearted mythical Buddhist monk Ji Gong. In one of his many heroic acts, he saved an entire town from certain death after he had a premonition of the town being buried by an avalanche.

Chi-you and His Repulsive Brothers

The legends surrounding the Yellow Emperor Huang-di recall his military skills and bravery. At the same time, the surviving accounts of his exploits go into a fair amount of detail about his chief adversary—Chi-you—who launched a massive invasion of China. The ancient sources say that that repulsive character was the oldest of seventy-two brothers, all of whom were misshapen and cruel in various ways. Historians O.B. Duane and N. Hutchison describe Chi-you and his siblings, saying that

> they each spoke the language of humans, but their bodies below the neckline were those of animals with cloven [split] feet. Their heads were made of iron and their hideous copper faces contained four repulsive eyeballs protruding from mottled foreheads. These brothers ate all kinds of food, but they particularly liked to eat stones and chunks of metal, and their special skill was the manufacture of battle weapons, including sharp lances, spears, axes, shields, and strong bows.

O.B. Duane and N. Hutchison, *Chinese Myths and Legends*. Brockhampton, 1998, pp. 36–37.

Several Different Types of Heroes

Huang-di's tales show that, like all ancient and medieval peoples, the Chinese revered heroic individuals of the past. Moreover, those memorable champions earned praise for embodying different virtues. University of Cambridge professor Anne Birrell asserts that Huang-di gained respect for displaying "acts of military courage, idealism, devotion to a cause, [and] nobility of spirit."[23] Moreover, she says, he is remembered not only as a warrior hero but also as a culture hero because of the several important inventions he introduced.

Among the other types of Chinese mythical heroes, Birrell says, were those who became famous as saviors of humanity. Nuwa, the goddess who created the first humans, also saved them by stopping the sky from collapsing on them. In addition, there was the archer Hou Yi, who shot nine of the original ten suns out of the sky, saving human civilization from fiery destruction.

Some other savior heroes are fondly remembered for providing humanity with an environment necessary for their survival

ZHU LONG
A large reptilian creature that supposedly created and maintained the cycle of day and night

and prosperity. Perhaps the best-known example is Zhu Long. A large reptilian creature made by the gods (or in some accounts divine himself), the ancient Chinese believed he created and maintained the relentless cycle of day and night. Ancient artists portrayed him as having red skin, Birrell points out, "with a snake's body and a human head. When he shuts his vertical eyes, it grows dark, and when he opens them it grows bright. . . . He has such care for the well-being of humans that he never eats, sleeps, or rests."[24]

A Modest Monk to the Rescue

Still another memorable mythical character in the savior hero category was a modest, kindhearted Buddhist monk named Ji Gong. Although he came from a wealthy family, as a young man he rejected the idea of wealth and privilege. Instead, he took a vow of poverty and dedicated himself to helping the poor and others in need. "There are many accounts of him healing the sick and fighting against injustice inflicted on the downtrodden,"[25] says Buddhist historian David Lai.

The best-known example of Ji Gong's heroic efforts to help people is a tale in which he supposedly prevented all the inhabitants of a town from dying in a sudden catastrophe. The myth, often titled "Ji Gong Abducts the Bride," became immensely popular over the centuries. As a result, in modern times it inspired numerous plays, ballets, novels, and even a Chinese television series.

One day Ji was riding his donkey from his mountain monastery to a nearby town, the story begins. Suddenly, seemingly out of nowhere, a fuzzy image formed in his mind, a disturbing scene in which that very town lay in ruins. Seconds later, he had a more vivid vision that the ground shook violently

JI GONG
A kindhearted monk famous for helping people in need or distress

Mulan's Ancient Ballad

Modern scholars estimate that the poem, or possibly folk song, titled *The Ballad of Mulan* was composed by an unknown author sometime during the 400s or 500s CE. It tells the myth of Mulan, who may or may not have been a real person, in fair detail. In the following excerpts, she explains why she decided to enlist in the army, while a narrative voice tells how she both armed herself and left her family behind.

> Father has no grown-up son,
> Mulan has no elder brother.
> I want to buy a saddle and horse,
> And serve in the army in Father's place. . . .
> In the East Market she buys a spirited horse,
> In the West Market she buys a saddle,
> In the South Market she buys a bridle,
> In the North Market she buys a long whip.
> At dawn she takes leave of Father and Mother.
> In the evening camps on the Yellow River's bank.
> She doesn't hear the sound of Father and Mother calling.
> She only hears the Yellow River's flowing water cry tsien tsien [onomatopoeic noise of a running river].

Quoted in Han H. Frankel, *The Flowering Plum and the Palace Lady: Interpretations of Chinese Poetry.* Yale University Press, 1976, pp. 68–72.

and the top of a nearby mountain broke off, tumbled downhill, and crushed the town.

Realizing it was a premonition, the anxious monk rushed to the town and ran from street to street. Everyone must flee at once, he cried out as loud as he could. If they remained, he added, they would perish in a massive avalanche. Seeing that it was a quiet, windless day, however, almost no one paid any attention to these warnings. In desperation, therefore, Ji searched for an alternate way to evacuate the citizenry. Mere seconds later, he noticed a crowd of wedding guests marching along the street on their way to the local church. Thinking quickly, he hurried to the bride, slung her over his shoulder, and ran away as fast as his stubby legs could move.

Just as Ji had hoped, the groom thought his fiancée was being kidnapped and bolted after the monk. The other marchers swiftly followed, and soon everyone in the town joined in the chase. Once the pursuit passed the town's main gate, a tremendous crash echoed through the surrounding hills. The townspeople spun around just in time to witness the peak of the closest mountain break away and plunge downward. They watched in horror, helpless to intervene, as the avalanche flattened every structure in the town. In a moment of clarity and huge expression of relief, all present realized that Ji was their savior, not an abductor. And they, along with future generations of Chinese, never forgot his clever and selfless display of heroism.

The Most Accomplished Monster Killer

Some Chinese hero narratives featured monster slayers, with feats of daring and strength similar to the famous Greek strongman Heracles (today better known as Hercules). Perhaps the most accomplished of the Chinese monster killers was Hou Yi, who had already distinguished himself by eliminating all but one of the original ten suns. The reigning emperor, Yao, next called on the savior Hou Yi to rid the earth's surface of three horrifying creatures. Those beasts roamed freely, reputedly killing hundreds of people and posing dire threats to entire towns.

One of the most dangerous of the monsters was an enormous serpent that lived in a lake near the Yangtze River, which runs eastward through central China. Week after week there were reports of the beast capsizing boats and devouring the fishers who struggled to survive in the deep water. To attract the serpent's attention, Hou Yi took a small boat out on the river and rowed it back and forth. This plan worked because the creature soon arrived on the scene. According to Tao Tao Liu Sanders:

> The monster's ugly head appeared first, its serpent body coiling out behind it as it raced towards its prey. Yi shot arrow after arrow into its scaly skin, but the serpent was

> strong and eventually Yi had to fight it at close quarters from his tiny, rocking boat. At last, with a thrust of his sword, he pierced its heart. With a last thrust of its tail, the serpent disappeared forever beneath the water.[26]

Having eliminated the lake serpent, Yi tracked down and slew the other two monsters. One was a giant bird that swooped down and grabbed people, carried them off to its huge nest, and ate them alive. Hou Yi attached a long rope to the back of an arrow and shot the shaft into the beast's hide. Then he forcefully yanked on the rope, pulling the bird onto the ground, where he used his dagger to cut its throat. Not long after dispatching this monster, Hou Yi attacked and killed a colossal, people-eating boar.

A Female Hero's Moving Story

Although the celebrated myths of Hou Yi, Ji Gong, and Haung-di involve male protagonists, not all Chinese heroes were male. Perhaps the most famous Chinese heroine was Hua Mulan, usually more simply called Mulan. Her inspirational and moving story originated in the period from 386 to 534 CE, when China was ruled by the Northern Wei dynasty. Often, the Wei rulers were compelled to go to war against an invading Mongolian people called the Rouran.

MULAN
The most renowned Chinese female mythical hero, she pretended to be a man and fought in the army

During those conflicts, the Wei government ordered every Chinese family to contribute at least one male fighter to serve in the dynasty's army. The patriotic Mulan, then in her late teens, very much wanted her own family to take part. The problem, she realized, was that her father was aged and lame, and his only son was just six years old. Mulan decided to fight in her father's and brother's stead. To disguise herself, she donned men's armor and gathered the weapons her father had used in his young manhood.

Mulan managed to enlist in the army. And in the months and years that followed, she traveled far and wide and fought just as effectively and valiantly as the male soldiers. A written work of that period, *The Ballad of Mulan*, has survived. In it, Mulan ignores the calls to remain at home and instead travels "ten thousand miles on the business of war." During a period of twelve years, the poem states, she "saw Generals die in a hundred battles"[27] while she persevered. Eventually, she was rewarded by the emperor for her service, and she asked only for a horse to carry her

The famous Chinese heroine Mulan managed to enlist in the army in place of her aging father and young brother. In the years that followed, she traveled far and wide and fought just as effectively and valiantly as the male soldiers.

home. When she finally returned to her mother and father, she discarded her armor and weapons and put on her old clothes. In the generations that followed, Mulan and her bold actions became a legend in China.

According to University of Gdańsk historian Natalia Klimczak, modern scholars still debate whether Mulan's myth is based in fact. She may or may not have been a real person, they say. However, Klimczak points out, to most Chinese the truth of the story is unimportant. For many centuries her story has served as an inspiration, and her character "has remained a very popular motif [theme] in art and literature. She appears as a heroine of more than ten movies and theater plays," says Klimczak. To the Chinese, she is a beloved "symbol of bravery and honor . . . and as long as she inspires them, [her historical reality will] not matter to them."[28]

CHAPTER FIVE

Dragons, Foxes, and Other Creatures

There was a time in the dimly remembered past, ancient legends claim, when China and the rest of the world had no rivers or lakes yet. As a result, people and animals had to rely on rain for one of the most precious of resources—water. These conditions worked well enough until history's first known major drought struck. For almost a year, no rain fell, and untold numbers of humans and animals perished from thirst and starvation.

The gods saw what was happening, and some of them wanted to try to remedy the situation by causing rain to fall. But none dared to do so without first asking permission from the chief deity—the Jade Emperor. And because he was extremely busy at the time, it was close to impossible to obtain an audience with him.

Meanwhile, four friendly dragons who lived in a castle in the Eastern Sea (now the Pacific Ocean) saw the terrible drought unfold, and the death toll deeply concerned them. Their names were the Long Dragon, the Yellow Dragon, the Black Dragon, and the Pearl Dragon. Hoping to help end the ongoing disaster, they too asked for an audience with the Jade Emperor, and due to the immense respect he had for dragons, he made an exception and met with them.

During that conference, the dragons asked the master of heaven why he had not intervened and brought badly needed rain. His answer was that he had been extremely busy of late. After apologizing for the oversight, he promised to end the drought soon. However, after the dragons had departed his palace, the Jade Emperor got involved in some pressing administrative matters and forgot about his promise to make it rain.

When several days elapsed and no rain fell, the four frustrated dragons made a fateful decision. They boldly chose to end the drought themselves. Leaping into the air, they flew out over the sector of the sea near their home, and each scooped up tremendous amounts of water in their mouths. Then they soared over

During a terrible drought, four dragons sought permission from China's chief deity, the Jade Emperor (pictured), to remedy the problem. When he failed to act, they intervened.

the earth's land portions, releasing the life-giving liquid a little at a time. People everywhere were both relieved and thrilled, and many of them sang hymns of thanksgiving.

One individual who was not at all pleased with the dragons' intervention was a sea god who worried that they had removed too much water from the oceans. He complained to the Jade Emperor, who decided to punish the four flying heroes. The emperor responded by notifying a mountain deity, who imprisoned the four heroes in a massive cavern inside the mountain. This plan swiftly backfired, however. Summoning forth the magical powers that most dragons possessed, they caused huge torrents of water from deep underground to gush up onto the land. In so doing, they created China's four largest rivers. Thereafter, those plentiful water sources ensured that no single drought would ever destroy humanity. In the meantime, the floodwaters carried the heroes back out of the mountain, and they returned to their home in the sea.

Frequently Friendly Beings

The ancient Chinese were certainly not the only people of past ages who perpetuated myths about dragons. The ancient Greeks and Babylonians and the medieval Germans and Norse were but a few of those who told tales about dragons or dragon-like creatures. Most of these stories, though, depicted dragons as monstrous and threatening. They were wicked antagonists in tales that featured heroes who were strong and clever enough to track down and slay such mighty reptilian beasts.

In stark contrast, the ancient Chinese saw most dragons as beneficial, helpful, and frequently friendly beings. In fact, the archetype, or model, for the Chinese dragon, called a *long*, was a big, strong, often compassionate creature that usually got along well with humans. It was "intensely noble," says Tao Tao Liu, and a "largely benign spirit that dwelt in the sky [or underwater]."[29]

The ancient Chinese believed that many dragons brought good luck. And, like the four heroes who ended the drought, Liu adds,

The Uniqueness of Chinese Dragons

Mythical Chinese dragons possessed several distinctive physical traits that made them different from dragons in other national mythologies. As former Wadham College professor Tao Tao Liu Sanders explains, a Chinese dragon, or *long*,

> breathed not fire, but clouds, and has been described [in ancient texts] as having the head of a camel, the horns of a stag, the eyes of a demon, the ears of a cow, the neck of a snake, the belly of a clam, the scales of a carp, the claws of an eagle, and the paws of a tiger. Very often, however, he appeared in human form. His element was water and he controlled rainfall as well as the water in rivers, lakes, and streams. Unlike the dragon of European mythology, he was usually a well-meaning creature. . . . Each sea, river, or lake had its guardian dragon, often of kingly status, living in a crystal underwater palace surrounded by priceless treasures. Though he guarded his treasure jealously from thieves, he occasionally gave a share to a mortal who had pleased him in some way.

Tao Tao Liu Sanders, *Dragons, Gods, and Spirits from Chinese Mythology*. Bedrick, 1994, p. 48.

they "symbolized water, which nourished the land and allowed Chinese civilization to flourish."[30] Thus, it was common for Chinese dragons to help communities and entire kingdoms prosper.

The Mother, the Boy, and the Pearl

Another common trait of Chinese dragons—also frequently seen in Norse dragon tales—is the ability to undergo a fantastic physical transformation, in which a dragon becomes a person or a person transforms into a dragon. One of the most memorable Chinese myths in which a human turns into a dragon is often titled "The Dragon's Pearl." In it, a woman and her teenaged son were poor and lived in a humble one-room hut. They were able to just barely survive thanks to the son's job: he cut down patches of tall grass that he sold to farmers to feed their livestock.

When the boy was sixteen, a terrible drought struck, and most of the grass in the area withered and died. So he had little to sell, and soon he and his mother were at the brink of starvation. One day when he was desperately searching for any surviving grass, he found a splendid rose-colored pearl. Initially, he and his mother planned to sell it. But then they witnessed its miraculous power. When the pearl was placed beside a grain of rice, a multitude of new rice grains appeared out of nowhere. Hoping its multiplication magic would work on other objects, Tao Tao Liu Sanders writes, that night the boy and his mother "put the pearl in the box where they kept their money and, sure enough, the next morn-

In the myths of many cultures, dragons were seen as terrifying monsters. The people of ancient China saw dragons in a different light. They considered them to be noble and compassionate creatures.

ing the box was overflowing with coins. Then they tried the bottle where they kept their lamp oil, and the next day it was full of the best-quality oil. Using the pearl carefully, the mother and son became quite wealthy."[31]

With the family's sudden good fortune, the son grew lazy and careless, and one day he accidentally swallowed the pearl. Soon, to his mother's horror, his body began to change in strange ways. Horns appeared on his head, his skin sprouted scales, and his eyes turned into yellow slits. Within a few hours, he had transformed into a huge dragon, and much to his mother's regret, he spent the rest of his life—like many dragons—guarding rivers and other water sources.

Always Be Wary of Foxes

Although many ancient Chinese legends feature dragons—beings that came to symbolize China's emperors and the nation's civilization—the fox appears more prevalently in ancient Chinese animal tales. Some modern scholars attribute the widespread appearance of the fox in ancient stories to its elusive nature. Foxes tend to be depicted as cunning, stealthy, and quick, aligning them with mystical trickster spirits.

As deceptive spirits, foxes—like dragons—were thought to possess the power to shape-shift, often assuming human form to trick or otherwise take advantage of people. The selfish and mischievous fox goddess, Huxian, was also a legendary shape-shifter. As a divine being her true form was invisible and spirit-like, but she preferred the feel of a flesh-and-blood body, so she often assumed human form, usually to fool or manipulate people she encountered.

One of that deity's favorite human forms was that of an attractive young woman. This was because it allowed her to more easily tease or deceive men. In one of her best-known myths, for example, one day she was floating near the earth's surface in her invisible

HUXIAN
The Chinese fox goddess, who often shape-shifted into the form of a young woman

divine form. Suddenly, she noticed an unusually handsome young man. Attracted to him, she swiftly transformed into a beautiful maiden and introduced herself.

The two spent more than two weeks together, day and night, and the young man fell deeply in love with her. During that time, however, Huxian quickly grew bored with him, as she had with many other men in the past. Finally, she rather curtly told him that the romance was over. Devastated, he became deeply depressed and remained heartbroken for the rest of his life. The main moral of this story, the ancient Chinese felt, was that people should always be wary of and never trust foxes.

The Headless Giant

While dragons might help humans and foxes might toy with them, neither was malevolent. However, plenty of frightening and deadly creatures populated China's myths.

Of the Chinese monster myths, one of the more often retold is that of the so-called Headless Giant, Xing Tian. Though humanlike, Xing Tian was much larger and considerably deformed. He joined the army of the barbaric Chi-you, the foreign invader who opposed the Yellow Emperor.

XING TIAN
Better known as the Headless Giant, he was defeated in single combat by the Yellow Emperor

At one point during the war against Huang-di, Xing Tian approached China's imperial palace and loudly challenged the emperor to single combat. To the surprise of the Chinese soldiers, the emperor accepted that challenge and marched out to meet the misshapen giant. After they had fought for an hour, Huang-di caught Xing Tian off guard and managed to slice off his head. As O.B. Duane and N. Hutchison tell it, "A terrifying scream escaped the gaping, bloody mouth of the giant as his head began to topple forward, crashing with a loud thud to the ground."[32]

Xing Tian's body then panicked and started searching for the head. But the emperor wisely buried that lost appendage in a faraway place where it could never be found. For many succeeding

The Thousand Mile Horse

Although most Chinese creature myths relate cautionary stories about majestic dragons, wily foxes, or scary monsters, a few teach more charming lessons. The story of the Thousand Mile Horse is one of those tales. It begins when a solider discovers to his amazement that his horse can run a thousand miles in a single day. Moreover, the animal could move quickly and with little effort. The soldier eventually died in battle, but the horse survived. First, a farmer bought the steed, and later it was passed on to a horse trainer. Both men unwisely fed the horse far less food than it needed to remain in good health. So it was unable to run very far, which frustrated its owners, who had heard of its fabulous endurance. The horse changed hands again, this time to the head groom of the reigning emperor. The stableman, who smartly understood the horse's need for proper nutrition, fed the animal enough energy-filled foods. To the emperor's delight, the well-fed creature took him on a rollicking, joyful thousand-mile ride each day for many years. The moral of the tale is that talent exists in people or beasts, but it must be recognized and nurtured.

centuries, the story goes, the giant's body roamed the countryside on dark nights searching in vain for its head and killing any person who got in the way.

Other Scary Characters

Some ancient Chinese refused to leave home after dark for fear of meeting up with the marauding giant. Yet he was by no means the scariest creature said to be lurking in dark places. Considerably more horrifying was the *taotie*. According to Ken Liu, a well-known translator of Chinese tales into English, the taotie was "an extremely greedy beast with an outsized head. It [was] so ravenous [extremely hungry] that it ultimately swallowed the rest of its own body, leaving behind only a head. The very name of taotie has become a synonym in Chinese for a glutton."[33] The taotie's image cautioned against overindulgence and could easily strike fear in the hearts of those who even viewed its form in bronze castings of the legendary monster.

TAOTIE
A vicious, scary creature that eats its own body, leaving behind only the head

Another widely feared Chinese mythical monster was the *jiangshi*. An undead being, it was in many ways a cross between a zombie and a vampire. Said to raid isolated farms and villages, it was known to seek out and devour human babies. In some stories it attacked adults and somehow drained their life forces, leaving their bodies shriveled and quite dead.

Perhaps the most widely feared beings in Chinese mythology are ghosts. In fact, in China ghosts are frequently seen as no less repulsive and frightening than vampires and werewolves are in

According to myth, the undead being known as a jiangshi *(pictured) raided isolated farms and villages in its search for human babies to devour. When it attacked an adult, it drained the victim's life force and left behind a shriveled corpse.*

European, American, and other Western lore. But they are not simply fictional phantoms in books and movies. Like the ancient Chinese, many of China's modern residents firmly believe that the spirits of deceased people regularly haunt and at times try to harm the living.

Especially scary in China is a dangerous kind of ghost called the Nu Gui, roughly translated as "vengeful female ghost." In surviving myths, the ghost women's husbands badly wronged them when they were alive, and now they have returned to seek revenge. The general belief is that because ghost women were abused by men, they kill only males, sparing women.

The moral dimension to the ghost women's tales is common to most Chinese myths. For example, most Chinese dragon tales promote the idea that it is ethical to care about society and help it survive. And the fox myths are in part warnings to be wary of those who lie and try to manipulate others.

Thus, say the editors of the Chinese online site GoEast Mandarin, the myths about ancient Chinese creatures are more than merely fanciful and entertaining. Those tales also "reflect the fundamental beliefs, values, and wisdom that have shaped Chinese civilization over millennia." The many colorful Chinese creature stories offer "a profound window into the spiritual, philosophical, and ethical underpinnings of a great culture."[34]

SOURCE NOTES

Introduction: In Harmony with Nature

1. O.B. Duane and N. Hutchison, *Chinese Myths and Legends*. Brockhampton, 1998, p. 10.
2. Te Lin, *Chinese Myths*. McGraw-Hill, 2001, p. 14.
3. Duane and Hutchison, *Chinese Myths and Legends*, p. 12.

Chapter One: How the World and People Came to Be

4. Lihui Yang and Deming An, *Handbook of Chinese Mythology*. Oxford University Press, 2005, pp. 63–64.
5. E.C. Rammel, "Pangu: Mythological Insights into the Chinese Creation Story," Ancient Origins, March 27, 2024. www.ancient-origins.net.
6. Tao Tao Liu Sanders, *Dragons, Gods, and Spirits from Chinese Mythology*. Bedrick, 1994, p. 13.
7. Yang and An, *Handbook of Chinese Mythology*, pp. 67–68.
8. Sanders, *Dragons, Gods, and Spirits from Chinese Mythology*, p. 16.
9. Quoted in Tao Tao Liu, *The Chinese Myths: A Guide to the Gods and Legends*. Thames and Hudson, 2022, p. 80.

Chapter Two: A Vast Pantheon of Divine Beings

10. Quoted in Time-Life Books, *Land of the Dragon: Chinese Myth*. Time-Life, 1999, p. 125.
11. Quoted in Time-Life Books, *Land of the Dragon*, p. 104.
12. Quoted in Time-Life Books, *Land of the Dragon*, p. 105.
13. Quoted in Time-Life Books, *Land of the Dragon*, pp. 105–106.
14. Duane and Hutchison, *Chinese Myths and Legends*, p. 76.
15. Emily Mark, "Most Popular Gods & Goddesses of Ancient China," *World History Encyclopedia*, April 25, 2016. www.worldhistory.org.
16. Mark, "Most Popular Gods & Goddesses of Ancient China."
17. Mark, "Most Popular Gods & Goddesses of Ancient China."

Chapter Three: Timeless Tales of Mythic Lovers

18. Quoted in Time-Life Books, *Land of the Dragon*, p. 79.
19. *China Daily*, "Classic Love Stories from China," March 15, 2011. www.chinadaily.com.cn.

20. Yang Tingting, "Ancient Love Tales," World of Chinese, October 28, 2020. www.theworldofchinese.com.
21. Victoria Ma, "Chinese Valentine's Day," Chinese Historical & Cultural Project. https://chcp.org.

Chapter Four: Celebrated Warriors and Other Heroes

22. Duane and Hutchison, *Chinese Myths and Legends*, p. 37.
23. Anne Birrell, *Chinese Myths*. University of Texas Press, 2000, p. 38.
24. Birrell, *Chinese Myths*, p. 42.
25. David Lai, "Ji Gong—the Crazy Monk of China," Tsem Rinpoche, September 29, 2016. www.tsemrinpoche.com.
26. Sanders, *Dragons, Gods, and Spirits from Chinese Mythology*, p. 28.
27. Quoted in Han H. Frankel, *The Flowering Plum and the Palace Lady: Interpretations of Chinese Poetry*. Yale University Press, 1976, p. 70.
28. Natalia Klimczak, "The Dramatic True Story Behind Disney's *Mulan*," Ancient Origins, May 29, 2020. www.ancient-origins.net.

Chapter Five: Dragons, Foxes, and Other Creatures

29. Liu, *The Chinese Myths*, p. 128.
30. Liu, *The Chinese Myths*, p. 128.
31. Sanders, *Dragons, Gods, and Spirits from Chinese Mythology*, p. 59.
32. Duane and Hutchison, *Chinese Myths and Legends*, p. 46.
33. Ken Liu, "5 Chinese Mythological Creatures That Need to Appear in More SF/F," *B&N Reads* (blog) April 12, 2016. www.barnesandnoble.com.
34. GoEast Mandarin, "6 Most Popular Chinese Mythical Creatures and Their Meanings." https://goeastmandarin.com.

FOR FURTHER RESEARCH

Books

Earline Carothers, *Dragon Dynasty: Mysteries of Chinese Mythology*. Published by the author, 2025.

Aaron Hwang, *Chinese Mythology: Legendary Tales of Heaven, Earth, Humanity, and Beyond*. Running Press Kids, 2024.

Jean K. Lee, *Chang'e: Goddess of the Moon*. ABDO, 2023.

Jiankun Sun, *Fantastic Creatures of the Mountains and Seas: A Chinese Classic*. Arcade, 2021.

Xiaobing Wang, *Myths of China*. Dorling Kindersley, 2024.

Yun Xian, *Ancient Chinese Myths*. Published by the author, 2024.

Internet Sources

Sauget Aghikari, "Top 10 Astonishing Ancient Chinese Mythology Stories," Ancient History Lists, April 22, 2024. www.ancienthistorylists.com.

Chinese Sage, "Dragons, Qilin, Phoenix and Other Mythical Beasts." www.chinasage.info.

CLI, "Chinese Dragons: Their Types, History, and Significance," October 29, 2024. https://studycli.org.

Wu Haiyun, "How Guan Yu Became China's God of War, Wealth, and Everything Else," Sixth Tone, August 13, 2020. www.sixthtone.com.

Sara Lynn Hua, "Five Chinese Ghosts That Are Absolutely Terrifying," *Tutor ABC Chinese* (blog), October 31, 2016. https://blog.tutorabcwchinese.com.

Ellen Lloyd, "Legend of the Eight Immortals Who Know the Secrets of Nature," Ancient Pages, May 21, 2016. www.ancientpages.com.

Emily Mark, "Ghosts in Ancient China," *World History Encyclopedia*, April 20, 2016. www.worldhistory.org.

Minjie Su, "The Butterfly Lovers: A Classic Chinese Love Story," Medievalists.net. www.medievalists.net.

Qiu G. Su, "A Guide to Ghost Month in China," ThoughtCo., June 15, 2018. www.thoughtco.com.

Edward T.C. Werner, “Myths and Legends of China: Fox Legends,” Sacred Texts. www.sacred-texts.com.

World Stories, “The Story of Niu Lang and Zhi Nu.” https://worldstories.org.uk.

Ced Yong, “88 Mythical Chinese Characters to Know About,” Owlcation, January 27, 2025. https://owlcation.com.

Kuan L. Yong, “108 Chinese Mythological Gods and Characters to Know About,” Owlcation, March 12, 2025. https://owlcation.com.

Websites

Ancient China for Kids, Ducksters
www.ducksters.com/history/china/ancient_china.php
This highly useful website contains dozens of links to separate articles about Chinese history, culture, and myths.

Ancient Chinese Stories, Fables, and Legends for Kids
https://china.mrdonn.org/stories.html
This site, geared to young readers, features dozens of short retellings of ancient Chinese fables.

Chinese Mythology, Godchecker
www.godchecker.com/chinese-mythology
Conceived by the late modern mythologist Chas Saunders, this informational site introduces the best-known ancient Chinese gods in a well-designed, eye-catching format. Numerous links lead to separate articles about those deities.

INDEX

PICTURE CREDITS

Cover: yienkeat/Shutterstock

4: Shutterstock.com
6: BLUR LIFE 1975/Shutterstock
10: Jesus Giraldo Gutierrez/Shutterstock
13: John Astor/Alamy Stock Photo
17: Science History Images/Alamy Stock Photo
20: Ivy Close Images/Universal Images Group/Newscom
23: Chronicle/Alamy Stock Photo
27: Pictures From History/Newscom
31: CPA Media Pte Ltd/Alamy Stock Photo
33: Dorling Kindersley ltd/Alamy Stock Photo
35: Tatiana Liubimova/Shutterstock
39: Science History Images/Alamy Stock Photo
40: TNIOH KOCK THAI/Shutterstock
46: Lebrecht Music & Arts/Alamy Stock Photo
49: Pictures From History/Newscom
52: © Archives Charmet/Bridgeman Images
56: Steve Lillie/Alamy Stock Photo

ABOUT THE AUTHOR

Classical historian and award-winning author Don Nardo has written numerous acclaimed volumes about ancient civilizations and peoples. They include more than four dozen overviews of the mythologies of the Sumerians, Babylonians, Egyptians, Greeks, Romans, Persians, Celts, Aztecs, Norse, Chinese, Japanese, and others. Nardo, who also composes and arranges orchestral and chamber music, lives with his wife Christine in Massachusetts.